All Piggies Great & Small

The guide to all things Guinea Pig brought to you by Lancashire Guinea Pig Rescue

By Danni Whitehead
www.lancashireguineapigrescue.com
Email: Lancsguinearescue@gmail.com

Chapters

Weight Chart

Introduction

If you are reading this book you have either bought a Guinea pig or two or are thinking about adding a Piggie to your life.
Congrats!
Guinea pigs are one of the most friendliest, lovable and social small pets you can own. Suitable for children and adults alike, the Guinea Pig is a very popular pet.
Like all pets, Guinea Pigs need suitable food, access to clean water, a suitable clean house and a friend or two and lots of interaction.
If you are thinking about getting your child Guinea pigs just be aware that Piggies do need to be cleaned regularly and that can be hard work for young children so an adult must be prepared to help. A pet should not be the sole responsibility of a child, this is how many Piggies end up in rescues. Ask yourself do you have time and space for piggies? Can you care for a Piggie until the end of its life? Do you have the financial means to get a pet?
Be aware as well that many vets have only limited experience with Guinea Pigs, they are classed as an exotic pet in veterinary terms. Many of the medicines you will receive for Guinea Pigs will be dog or cat medicine.
With that in mind, please read on for more Piggie information.

Mavis
1 year
Female

Guinea Facts

Guinea Pigs, also known as Cavies, originally come from South America but can now be found worldwide. They are part of the rodent family, as their teeth constantly grow, and are descendants of Cavia cutleri. They are purely herbivores and love to forage. People of South America domesticated Guinea pigs as far back as 500 BCE, so they have always been a hit with people. They eventually came to Europe via the Spanish conquistadors and sold as exotic pets, even to royalty. The name Guinea Pig comes from their original price in England of one guinea and because they are said to look like little pigs. Many think it is because of their appetite. These little guys never stop eating and will wheek wheek for more.

Source: https://www.britannica.com/animal/guinea-pig

Male Guinea pigs are called a 'boar' and a female is called a 'sow'. Babies are known as pups.

Guinea Pigs can make a variety of sounds, the most well known is the 'wheek - wheek' sound. Owners will hear their Piggies make this sound when you rustle a bag or even open the fridge. They can also make a purring noise which is either contentment or fear, chatter their teeth and they can rumble, which is usually a dominance thing, known as a rumble strut. Some piggies can even whistle and chirp like birds.

Piggie diet

Piggies love to eat and can easily become obese or diabetic, apparently they have thousands of taste buds. A good starting point for owners is to fill a bowl up with Guinea pig nuggets (this gives Piggies vitamin C, like us they can not make their own vitamin C and will need it in their food), throwing away any that have not been eaten the day after. Pregnant and underweight Piggies can be given more.

Fresh vegetables / herbs / plants daily and always supply them with good quality hay daily such as Timothy hay. Hay should make up most of their diet as this is needed for digestion. Do not feed Pigs alfalfa hay unless directed by a vet as it is too high in protein and calcium and may cause kidney stones.

Fresh, clean water should be provided all the time. Piggies can be thirsty so bottles may have to be topped up twice a day. Bottles are generally better than bowls as Piggies tend to knock over bowls and flick poo and sawdust etc in it.

To get the most out of their herbivore diet, Guinea Pigs will eat their own poo. They will do two types of poo, a soft one that they will eat, which is semi digested plant fibre and then the hard pellets you will see dotted about the cage. Because the Guinea Pigs only eat the semi digested poo, this is known as cecotrophy. The Piggies will in a sense, eat their food twice.

Small, teardrop shaped poo can be a sign of dehydration and that the Piggie is not eating enough.

If the visible poos are soft, withholding vegetables until they harden again can help.

Source: https://nibbleandgnaw.com/blogs/news/what-do-guinea-pigs-eat

Piggie Menu

- Leafy green lettuce
- Kale
- Fennel
- Corn on the Cob / Baby Corn
- Romaine Lettuce
- Peas
- Basil
- Artichokes
- Greed and red bell peppers
- Cucumber
- Beetroot (will create red poo)
- Broccoli
- Brussel Sprouts (even though not many Piggies are fans of the sprout)
- Spinach
- Sweet Peppers
- Celery
- Cress
- Lambs Lettuce
- Dill
- Parsley

- Rocket
- Swiss Chard
- Turnips
- Watercress
- Coriander
- Dandelions (All is safe to eat)
- Cauliflower leaves
- Courgette

Treats

- Tomatoes
- Cranberries
- Grapes
- Butternut Squash
- Cabbage & Cauliflower (in moderation as these vegetables are very gassy and Guinea Pigs can not get rid of the extra gas)
- Strawberries
- Banana
- Apple
- Pears
- Bok Choy
- Blueberries
- Kiwi
- Papaya
- Pumpkin
- Peaches
- Melon
- Carrots
- Orange

No thanks

- Meat (Piggies are strictly herbivores)
- Dairy
- Lawn Mower clippings (they will bloat)
- Onions
- Corn Kernels
- Peanut Butter
- Potatoes
- Treats with honey or seed in them
- Chocolate
- Garlic
- Avocado
- Onions
- Leeks
- Mushrooms
- Nuts (too high in fat)
- Apple seeds (contains arsenic)
- Beans
- Rhubarb
- Chives
- Leaves of tomato and potato plants
- Iceberg Lettuce (can be given in moderation but has no nutritional value and high water content, causing bloating.)

Guinea Pigs, like us, can not make their own vitamin C so will need it from their nuggets and from leafy greens. Fruits like oranges can be given as a supplement. You can buy liquid vitamin C but it is not a reliable source of Vitamin C.

Make sure any weeds from outside are washed and safe to eat. If in doubt whilst picking weeds and plants, don't give it to the Piggies.

For undernourished Guinea Pigs, pregnant Piggies and Piggies with dental issues, a smoothie of nuggets, tomatoes, celery, banana, selective recovery powder and a teaspoon of sugar all blended together with water will help to get their strength back.

Bonding with your Piggie

Guinea Pigs can be skitty, flighty animals as they are a prey animal and are constantly looking for threats. It is normal for a Guinea Pig to want to hide and run away when you try to pick them up. An owner needs to show the Piggies that they are not a threat.

Try keeping your Piggies somewhere where they can see you and get used to you. Try handing them their favourite veg or fruit. Make it smaller each time so the Piggie will come closer to you. Talk to them gently so they can get used to the sound of your voice, they don't have the best of visions so may not be able to see you.
To get your Piggie used to you at first try picking the Piggie up whilst they are in a tunnel or snuggle pouch, this will lessen the Piggies fear if it starts running around the cage.

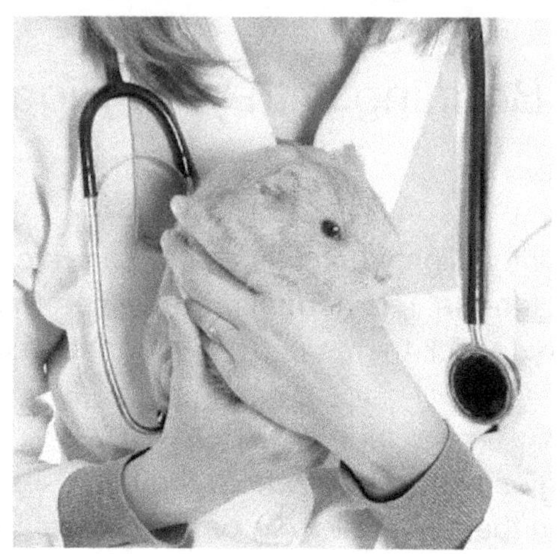

Source: https://www.brookvets.co.uk/handling-your-guinea-pig/

To pick up your Piggie, place one hand over them and use the other hand to scoop them up. They probably will try to run away when your hands loom over them, so hold them gently but firmly. Place them on your knee with a fleece under them as they may poo and wee on you but stay close to the floor in case they decide to jump off.

Set Ups

There are many different set ups for Piggies available, outdoor and indoor. Outdoor hutches will need extra protection in the winter such as hutch covers and heat pads for the piggies. Piggies hate the cold and also the heat. In summer, cool pads can be used to keep Piggies cool in their hutches and make sure there are places they can hide in the shade. Outdoor hutches and runs must be kept secure and predator proof.

Source:
https://www.omlet.us/shop/guinea_pig_products/outdoor_guinea_pig_run/

For an indoor cage the minimum a cage should be for two piggies is 76 x 127cm (30 x 50 inch). That is just the minimum, bigger is better and if you add to your herd, the cage must be bigger. For each new Piggie an area of 7.5 square feet must be added. Cages can be single tier, double and triple tier. Multi level cages are best if you are short on space.

C and C cages are a favourite with indoor piggies. They are small grids that are connected together with a corrugated plastic floor. These can be made into any shape and size you want and even add floors to them. Use cable ties to make them more secure.

Source: https://squeakdreams.com/guinea-pig-indoor-cc-and-diy-cages-2020-can-you-build-and-design-your-own-custom-cage/

Piggies love to hide, tunnels, wooden bridges and plastic hides are great for Piggies. If you have several Piggies make sure that each Piggie has a place to hide otherwise they will all squeeze into one small hide.

Piggies love soft beds and hides. They will poo loads in their beds and make a mess but they do enjoy being wrapped up in blankets in soft beds.

There are different substrates available, the most common being shavings. Some piggies can be allergic to shavings so other options are shredded paper, towels and fleece pads. Guineadad has some great fleeces perfect for Piggies.
And if you own Skinny or Werewolf Piggies then fleeces are a much better option than sawdust as they have delicate skin which can go dry.
Sawdust bedding will have to be changed regularly as it can become very dusty which the Piggies will be constantly breathing in as well as their own wee, poo and fur. This can lead to respiratory problems and also allergies with humans. Newspaper can be used to line cages and hutches but it can become soggy quickly. Puppy pads can be used too but your Piggies may chew them up. Hay can become damp too so will need to be changed every day. Hay racks and bags can be used to keep hay fresh for the Piggies to eat.

Cage freshener, which is a white powder, can be used in indoor hutches or cages to keep them smelling fresh.

Some owners choose to have free roaming Piggies, either in or outside. In both cases make sure the Piggies are secure and safe from other pets or predators. Piggies do love to roam but they will still need hides and tunnels to feel safe. And keep any wires away as Piggies will chew them. This goes for plants too as some can be toxic to Piggies.

It is best not to house them with rabbits as rabbits have powerful legs and can accidently harm the Piggies. They have different dietary needs, Rabbits can synthesise their own vitamin C but Guinea Pigs can't.
Rabbits can pass on respiratory disease to Guinea Pigs, as well as cats and dogs. If you do have Rabbits and Guinea Pigs living together, breaking them up could affect their welfare. It is best to neuter the Rabbit, feed separately and have a hiding place which is too small for the Rabbit to get in.

Source: https://www.birdexoticsvet.com/post/risks-guinea-pigs-rabbits-cohabitating

Grooming

All Piggies need basic grooming. This includes nail trimming, paw cleaning and moisturising, ear cleaning and a brush. Even short hair breeds will benefit from a quick brush and de-shed.

To trim a Piggies nail, one person holds the Piggie so its back is on your chest and holds its paws out whilst another person trims the nails. Only take the top white parts off, any lower and the nail will bleed. For Piggies with black nails, be very careful and just take the tips off. A light can be used to shine under the nail to show where the 'quick' is, which is the part that bleeds if cut too short. If you cut too short, don't worry, you can use pet safe antibacterial powder, just dip the nail in and it will stop the bleeding. Pet swabs can be used too. Corn flour can also be used if needed quickly.
Most piggies do not like their nails being cut so hold the piggies tight as they will squirm and squeak.

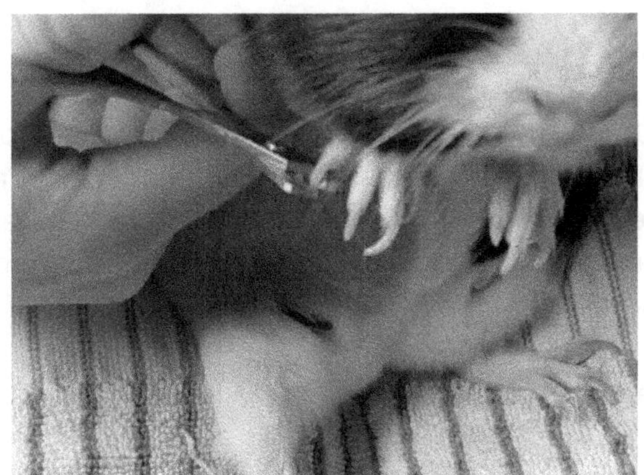

Source: https://surroundedbyanimals.co.uk/quick-guide-on-how-to-cut-guinea-pig-nails/

Whilst trimming the nails, check the feet. Piggies do not have pads on their feet. Their feet should be soft and pink. Sometimes Piggies can get very dry feet or in the case of the Piggies being on harsh flooring or damp bedding, Piggies can develop bumblefoot or pododermatitis. This is quite common. If a Piggie develops bumblefoot they will need a trip to the vets for antibiotics to stop any infections.
Obese Piggies are prone to this too. This can usually be cured by changing the bedding to something softer such as bedding hay or fleeces and changing their bedding more frequently. Urine scalds can harm a Piggies feet so bedding should be dry.
If left untreated, antibiotics may be needed. Worst case is amputation or euthansia. It is not contagious.

Guinea Pigs can develop 'spurs' on their feet which are hard bits of skin. These can be carefully clipped away, being careful not to cut too close to the skin as it will bleed.

Ears

Piggies can get dirty ears with burrowing in hay and bedding so carefully using a cotton wool stick, clean around the ears. Do not stick the cotton wool stick in their ear, just clean what you can see. The outer ear can be moisturised with coconut oil, baby oil or something similar. Piggies do have a bald patch behind the ears, this is normal.

Baths

Piggies can be bathed with an insecticidal Guinea Pig shampoo which helps keep mites at bay and also a waterless shampoo that acts as a deodoriser. Long hair breeds will need more grooming than short hairs and a hair trim. There are specialised small animal brushes and combs you can buy from pet shops and hair dressing scissors to trim their fur. Alternatively, take them to a Guinea Pig groomer.
We don't recommend using dog shampoo on Piggies as dogs and Pigs have different PH levels.

Source:
https://www.omlet.co.uk/guide/guinea_pigs/guinea_pig_health/baths_how_often/

Sweat Spot / Grease Gland

This grease gland is situated where a tail would be on the piggie. It is visible on both sexes and should be kept clean, with longer breeds it can become crusty. It is boars that will have the dirtiest sweat spot. It will feel slightly sticky, this is normal. It is used for marking territory.
Coconut oil can be used to break down extra grease and crustiness.
Grease glands can become infected so make sure checking the grease gland is part of a Guinea Pig's grooming routine.

Boar Glue

Boars can ejaculate over things, which can create a sticky mess, including over each other. A good groom is all that is needed.
Hardened glue inside the penis is not normal and may cause blockages when urinating.

Types

Guinea Pigs come in a variety of colours and types, each with their own set of characteristics. Take a look at the chart below of the different types of Guinea Pigs.

Source: https://helloralphie.com/types-of-guinea-pigs/

- The standard Guinea Pig is an American Guinea Pig, short hair with a great temperament. They are believed to be the oldest Guinea Pigs domesticated and there are around 20 different colours of American Guinea Pigs.

- Another favourite is the Abyssinian, recognisable by their swirly fur and friendly personality. They come in a lot of different colours and their swirls in their fur are known as rosettes. There are also Abyssinian Satin Piggies.

- A less common Piggie is the Alpaca Piggie with wavy, coarse fur. These do need to be brushed daily and are more high maintenance.

- An unusual breed is the Skinny Pig and the Baldwin Pig. The Baldwin Pig is completely hairless and skinny pigs have a bit of hair scattered around their nose and other parts of the body. These Piggies must be kept indoors, fed more than regular Piggies and always kept warm. They do love a nice, soft, warm blanket. Skinny pigs are prone to dry skin so should be moisturised with a friendly moisturiser like coconut oil.

- A Coronet Pig is another high maintenance Pig, it has long, flowing fur with no parting. This curious Piggie will need regular brushing and grooming.

- Himalayan Piggies are albinos with brown or black patches on their nose, ears and feet. They are born white and develop their marks or 'points' as they age. So called after the Himalayan cat. They do best indoors away from direct sunlight as their patches can fade in the sun and also when they are sick or scared. They have sensitive eyes due to being albino.

- The Lunkarya Piggie has long, rough curls. They are friendly Piggies that do not like the heat.

- Merino Piggies are lovable explorers. Their fur is curly and will need the occasional brush.

- The Peruvian Piggie has fur that can grow up to two foot in length and trail behind the piggie. Grooming and a trim is a must as the fur can grow over their heads into their faces. They are quite bold Piggies so may not be suitable for first time Guinea Pig owners.

- Rex Piggies are woolly, lovable Piggies with droopy ears. They do like to be petted and have curly whiskers.

- The Sheba or Yak Piggie has fur that sticks in every direction, it is a cross between an Abyssinian and a Peruvian Guinea PIg. These need daily grooming.

- Silkie / Sheltie Piggies have gorgeous locks that grow backwards. Maintenance is needed for these laid back Piggies.

- Teddy piggies only need an occasional brush and are very friendly Piggies. They tend to be smaller than other breeds. Also, Teddy Satin Piggies.

- The Texel Piggie is a cross between a Silkie and a Rex and is quite rare. They are known to be quite a calm breed.

- The White Crested Piggies are recognizable by the tuft of hair on their heads. Similar to the American breed, these Piggies are quite shy but will let you know when they are hungry.

- The Roan Guinea Pig has white hairs mixed with another solid colour. These must not be bred together as they create 'lethals', Piggies which wil have deformities.

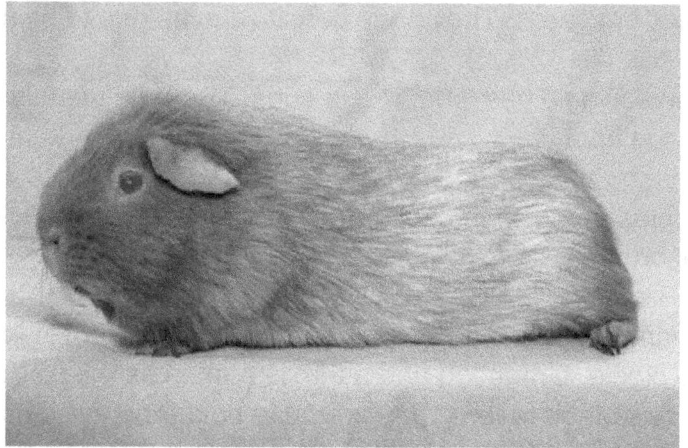

Source: https://www.britishcavycouncil.org.uk/Breeds/DRCC/

- Dalmatian Guinea Pigs have white hair with dark spots. Breeding two Dalmatians together can lead to the Piggies having deformities.
- Californian Guinea Pigs are similar to Himalayan Guinea Pigs but have dark eyes and come in black, chocolate, purple and beige points.

Socialising

Guinea Pigs are pack animals. They do enjoy being with each other.

Females can live together in large herds, boars can live in herds too as long as there's plenty of space. It has been done before but a pair of boars is usually the better option.
Sometimes, an older boar can live alone if they have failed numerous bonding sessions. But even if they have failed, you can keep trying to find them a friend as there is someone for everybody out there. Some success stories include pairing an older boar with a baby boar.

Most Piggies come in pairs.

It is possible to neuter your boar (if young enough) and have a neutered boar living with a harem of ladies. It is not ideal to spay a sow, the procedure is too invasive for their little bodies and not many vets will do the surgery.
Always keep an eye on your neutered boar after surgery, they can pull their sutures out and any hotness or swelling should be reported to the vet immediately.

Piggies do not need to be the same age to bond as older ones can get along with younger piggies. It is about matching Piggies personalities together.
Piggies should be bonded in neutral territory and supervised. Piggies may chase each other, mount and rumble at each other. This goes for both sexes. Piggies must be separated if they draw blood on each other. They can do pretty serious damage to each other with their teeth such as puncture wounds and ripped ears.

Sows that start chasing and mounting each other may have hormonal issues.

Source: https://www.pdsa.org.uk/taking-care-of-your-pet/looking-after-your-pet/small-pets/introducing-guinea-pigs

Health

Piggies can become ill with various ailments but most health issues are preventable with good husbandry. Being prey animals they can hide their illnesses well but there are some tell tale signs.

A Guinea Pig should have bright, alert eyes, no discharge from the nose, soft, pink feet, normal droppings and a healthy, full coat.
(Piggies can secrete a milky substance from their eyes which is used for grooming, this is normal)

Any changes to their eating habits or any weight loss is a cause for concern. PIggies can lose half their body weight in a matter of hours so they should be regularly weighed, once a week and also to check they are not getting too fat either.
A good weight for a boar is between 900 and 1200 grams and sows between 700 and 900 grams.
(Baby food is not suitable for Piggies!)
Not all antibiotics are safe for your Guinea Pig, always do your research. Any penicillin based antibiotics are dangerous to your Piggies. No vet should ever prescribe penicillin antibiotics for Piggies.
Baytril is a common medicine given to Piggies to treat infections. It is known to be harsh on the gut flora so a probiotic is recommended after administering Baytril. In some Piggies it can also reduce the appetite.

Avoid:

- amoxicillin (Clavamox)
- ampicillin
- bacitracin
- cefadroxil
- cephalexin * (derivative: Cefadroxil)
- cephalosporins
- cephazolin
- chlortetracycline
- clindamycin
- dihydrostreptomycin

- erythromycin
- lincomycin
- oxytetracycline
- penicillin
- streptomycin

Mites

Mites are little bugs that can burrow under the skin of Piggies and make them itchy. Most Guinea Pigs will have a small amount of parasites on them which generally do not cause any harm.
There are two types of Guinea Pig mites, Static mites (Chirodiscoides caviae) and Sarcoptic mange mites (Trixacarus Caviae).
Static mites live on the Piggies hair and sarcoptic mites can borrow under the skin.
Symptoms of a mite infestation are: excessive scratching, fur loss, scabs, thick, crusty skin, inflamed skin, lethargy, weight loss and seizures.
It is good to know what type of mites have infected your piggie before treating.
Insecticidal shampoo can be used and also a spot on pipette which can be bought from most pet shops for Guinea Pigs to keep mites away. The liquid is placed on the back of their neck. This contains ivermectin which helps against mange mites. Ivermectin does not kill the eggs so more treatment will be necessary. Selamectin does kill mites and the eggs.
Mange mites will not live on people but can cause dermatitis to people who have sensitive skin.
Mites can not be seen with the naked eye.
If your Guinea Pig is having seizures due to a mite infestation, wrap a bandage or similar around the Piggies body, which will control the seizures and stop the Piggie from further harm when having a seizure.
(Skin scrapings can give false negatives!)

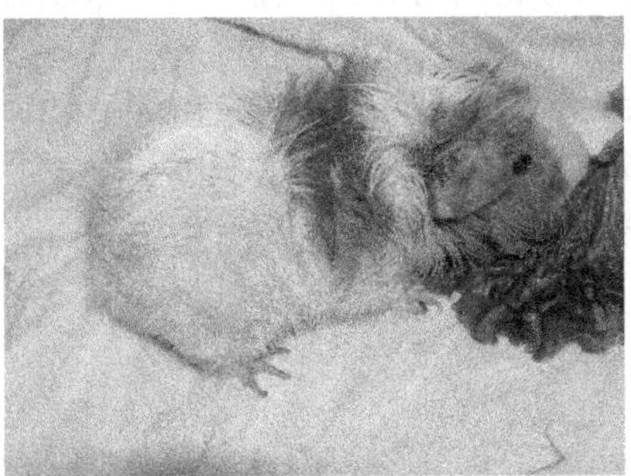

Source: https://guineapigconnection.typepad.com/pig_notes/2012/09/what-mites-do-to-guinea-pigs-part-i.html

Lice / Pediculosis

Lice can be seen moving on Guinea Pigs. They attach themselves to the Piggies hair shafts. The common types are: Oval lice (Gyropus Ovalis), Slender lice (Gliricola Lice) and Trimenopon hispidum. Lice needs to be treated straight away as it can spread to other piggies. The infestation will come noticeable when the Piggie is stressed. Ivermectin can usually treat lice infestations. Humans can not get Guinea Pig lice.

Fleas

Guinea Pigs can get fleas, as fleas will feed on any warm blooded animal. It is quite rare but if the Piggies are near other animals such as cats and dogs, fleas can jump to the Piggies. Make sure not to use dog or cat flea treatment but use Piggie friendly preventatives.

Flystrike / Myiasis

This can happen when bedding is soiled and becomes stuck to a Piggies rear end. Flies, such as green bottles and blow flies, are attracted to the mess and lay eggs on the Piggies. Maggots emerge and will eat the area and can cause toxic

shock. Many animals can suffer from flystrike, especially in summer so it is important to change bedding often.
Prevention is key by keeping a clean and dry environment.
There are over the counter products that can help protect against flystrike.
Piggies can survive flystrike if caught early enough.

Ringworm

Ringworm is a fungal infection that can be spread from Guinea Pig to Guinea Pig and can also be passed on to people. The main symptom is bald patches around the eyes, ears and nose but can spread to the back and legs. Anti fungal medicine can clear ringworm up in around six weeks.

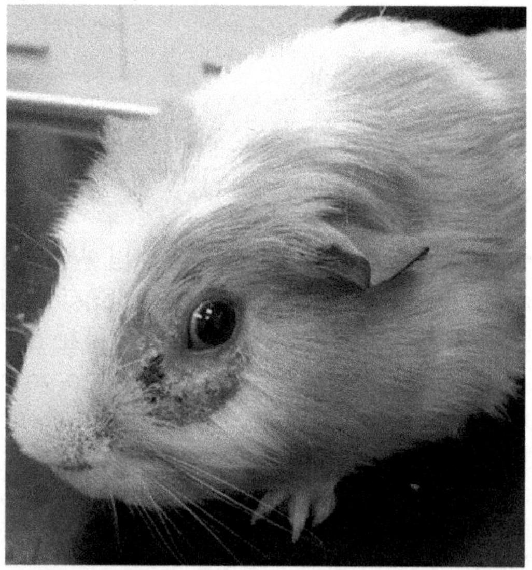

Source: https://www.theguineapigvet.co.uk/post/skin-parasites-and-fungal-infections-in-guinea-pigs

Barbering

Piggies can decide to give themselves and cage mates a haircut. If this occurs, the Piggies may need more stimulation, time in a run for example or more things to chew on.

Pregnancy Toxaemia (Ketosis)

This condition occurs when the Piggies body produces too many Ketones, which are a natural byproduct of the metabolism. Pregnant Guinea Pigs are prone to this as well as obese Piggies. There may be no signs of illness and a Piggie may die suddenly from this condition. A suitable diet is key to prevention and causing the least amount of stress to pregnant Piggies.

Osseus Metaplasia

This is when bone forms in soft tissue and muscle. It can be seen around the edge of the iris but if it grows over the iris it can cause visual impairment.

Impaction

This is quite common in older boars, they seem to lose function around their back end and poo can become stuck. This is usually the soft poo, the caecal pellets that Guinea Pigs eat. They may need a helping hand, gently pushing down near the anus will help push the impaction out. It will not smell pretty but will feel better for your piggie. This needs to be done regularly as the Piggie will not be getting the right nutrients from the caecal pellets and it can go mouldy inside the anus. This can also happen if Piggies are given the wrong food.

Neutered boars rarely develop impaction.

Cauliflower Willy

In some boars, it can appear that they have a ‘frilly willy’. This is generally nothing to worry about as the frill is actually the foreskin. As long as the penis can retract fully, this is quite a normal thing. The penis will have a white, creamy substance on it which is smegma, this keeps the shaft lubricated. A build up of smegma will need to be removed.

Teeth

The four front teeth should be even and the bottoms do look bigger than the tops. The molars should be even and any spurs that form on the teeth should be dealt with straight away by a vet as they can be quite painful. A piggie in pain will lose weight and struggle to eat, often dropping their food and dribbling on their chins.

If not fed the correct diet, piggies can develop painful dental issues. Their teeth constantly grow so they will need a high fibre diet to wear them down. Their teeth should be nice and white. Teeth do not need to be clipped.
Dental problems are a serious concern for Guinea Pigs and a vet trip will be needed asap. It is usually the molars which are harder to see that are the issue in dental problems.

Vitamin C deficiency

Guinea Pigs rely on their food for vitamin C as they can not produce it themselves. A poor diet can lead to vitamin C deficiency, signs are swollen joints, lethargy, anorexia, diarrhoea and a rough coat.

Urinary tract problems

These are common issues with Guinea Pigs, it can be avoided by not feeding a pig a diet high in calcium. They are prone to urinary stones and sows are more susceptible to cystitis. Symptoms include bloating, blood in the urine, a hunched body and problems with urination.
Urine can be cloudy, this is normal, but if it has a gritty texture this may mean there is sludge in the bladder.

Heart

A suspected URI that is not shifting with medication can be a sign of a heart problem instead. A vet can listen to a Piggie's heart and listen for any murmurs and check for pale membranes. An enlarged heart may not show up on an x-ray.

Piggies may make a 'hooting' sound and have other common conditions due to ill health such as respiratory problems, malocclusion and bumblefoot. A known symptom is necrosis of the tips of the ears which will change colour to black or white.

Gastrointestinal Stasis

If the bacterial flow of the gut becomes unbalanced in Piggies it can lead to 'Gut Stasis'. The Piggies can become bloated as toxins are released, causing diarrhoea and also death if left untreated. Internal parasites can also cause this.

Tumours, Cancer & Abscesses

Skin and mammary tumours are quite common, they can be benign (Lipoma) or malignant (Liposarcoma). Surgery is an option to remove tumours but Piggies don't always cope well with surgery and anaesthesia.

Trichofolliculoma is the most common lump in Piggies. It is a type of solid mass and can be removed surgically. It may appear scabby sometimes due to the Piggie biting at it.

Abscesses will need treatment such as surgery and antibiotics. Dental abscesses are hard to treat.

Lymphoma is the most commonly diagnosed cancer in Piggies.

Guinea Pigs can get leukaemia but fortunately it is rare.

Some diseases and bacteria can cause Cervical Lymphadenitis (CL) which are swellings and abscesses in the Piggie's neck. This can be contagious.

Cushing's Disease

This disease is caused by a hormonal imbalance and is not contagious to people or other Piggies.

Breathing problems (Upper Respiratory Infections)

Poor hygiene can lead to respiratory problems as well as bacteria such as Bordetella and Streptococcus. Piggies may also be carriers of the bacteria without it harming them.

Some Piggies may find sawdust too dusty so another bedding will have to be considered. Abnormal breathing should be investigated by a vet straight away. If your Piggie is making a crackling noise, then a vet trip is needed asap.

A symptom to look out for is crusty eyes.

Other treatments such as bronchodilators and oxygen can be given.

Eyes

Guinea Pigs should have round, slightly protruding eyes. They usually keep their eyes open during sleeping but some may close them fully. They do not blink. Guinea Pig eye colours come in dark, ruby and pink. A healthy eye will reflect red in a strong light, if it reflects white, the Piggie is probably blind. Guinea Pigs can excrete a milky discharge from their eyes which they then use for grooming purposes, this is normal.

Always check the eyes for any signs of injury or bits of hay that can work its way behind the eye, known as Hay Poke. A watery eye is a sign of this and a bluish film over the eye probably means the eye is ulcerated.

Crusty eyes and nose can be a sign of a respiratory issue which is often fatal to Piggies.

Guinea Pigs do not have the best vision so can easily adapt to being blind.

Microphthalmia is when the eye is really small or non-existent, making the Piggie blind.

'Blue Eye' can be caused by something irritating the eye like hay or hairs. Eye drops can usually sort the issue out if treated quick enough. If not treated it could turn into an ulcer or lead to the eye being removed. Some piggies do have naturally blue eyes.

Sunken eyes can be a sign of dehydration.

Nose

Fungal nose Stripe

This is quite common on Piggies, it appears as a white / yellow linear strip on the nose. This is usually not painful to the Piggie. It could be fungal in nature but seems not to respond to antifungal treatment. Coconut oil can be used to stop the dryness.

Ears

Ears should be checked regularly for dirt, mites and hay that can work its way into the ears. Shaking the head and a head tilt can be a sign of an ear infection. A Piggies temperature is regulated through the blood flow through the ears so it can look quite pink.
Ragged ear margins (around the ear) can be a sign of heart problems. Due to bad circulation it can cause necrosis on the tips of the ears. Piggies with pink ears have black round the edges and Piggies with black ears have white around the tips.

Lips

Crusty lips can be a sign of a bacterial lip infection. Fruits that are acidic such as tomatoes can aggravate the lips if fed too much.
Cheilitis is inflammation of the lips. Antibiotics and dental work can be used to treat this disorder. Coarse hay, excessive lip licking and sharp bits of food can cause sores which can become infected.

Fatty Eye / Pea Eye

This is a harmless, inherited condition that causes the conjunctival tissue beneath the eye to swell. If the eye starts to affect the Piggies vision then the Piggy will need to go to the vets. Usually, no treatment is needed for this.
Pea eye may also be caused by fluid build up due to poor circulation, so Piggies with heart conditions may be prone to Pea eye.

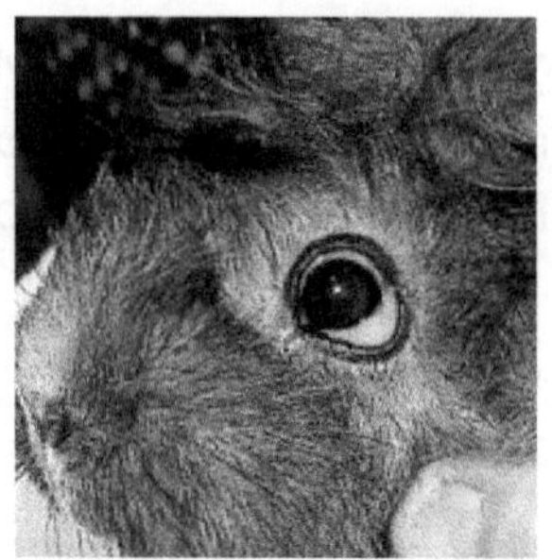

Source: http://www.guinealynx.info/eyes.htm

Lethal White Guinea Pigs

These are the offspring of mating Roan's together or Dalmatian breeds. They are born completely white due to having no skin pigmentation with red eyes. It is still possible to get pink eyed Piggies with white fur who are not 'Lethals'.
Lethals tend to have small, squinty eyes or they may be missing eyes altogether. Their lifespan is much shorter than a regular Guinea Pig and they would need constant vet checks, including dental work and being fed with a syringe.

Conjunctivitis

Conjunctivitis can be quite common in Piggies. It can be caused by an infection or from scurvy (lack of vitamin C). Eye drops and antibiotics can be given to treat this. Guinea pigs naturally have a small amount of white discharge that comes from the eyes to help groom but red, swollen eyes and greenish discharge is a sign of infection.

Zoonotic Diseases

These are diseases that can spread from animals to humans. Below are some diseases the Piggies can spread to people:

- Scabies
- Ringworm
- Salmonellosis
- Campylobacteriosis
- Yersiniosis
- Streptococcus

Boys Vs Girls

Sows

Sows are always the go to choice for first time Piggie owners. Sows rarely fight, even though some can bully the other and are generally easier to bond and can live in big herds.
Mother and daughter pairs are common but you do find that mother can be a bit of a bully, so the best pairs are either unrelated or sisters. Of course it does depend on each individual Guinea Pig.
Sows do not get impaction like boars do so this is a complication that will be avoided with sows.
Sows come into season every 15-17 days but don't bleed or cry like other animals.

Boars

Boars are usually more friendly and handable than sows, who remain quite skittish, even with age. There is a chance, however, of purchasing young boars and then when they enter their adolescent stage as we call it, around 12 months, they can fall out and start fighting. They then may need to be separated. This can happen but then a boar may bond better with another boar, most rescues offer a bonding service with Guinea Pigs.
Bonding can last several days and will continue for weeks after so supervision is needed.
It is not recommended to have more than two boars together, eventually they will fight with each other and can cause damage. However, we have had trio's and even a quad of boars that lived happily together.

Boars do not smell any more than sows do, if anything we have found sows can be very messy.
Older boars can get impaction where their back ends start to weaken and their poo will become stuck in their bottoms. It is always recommended to check and

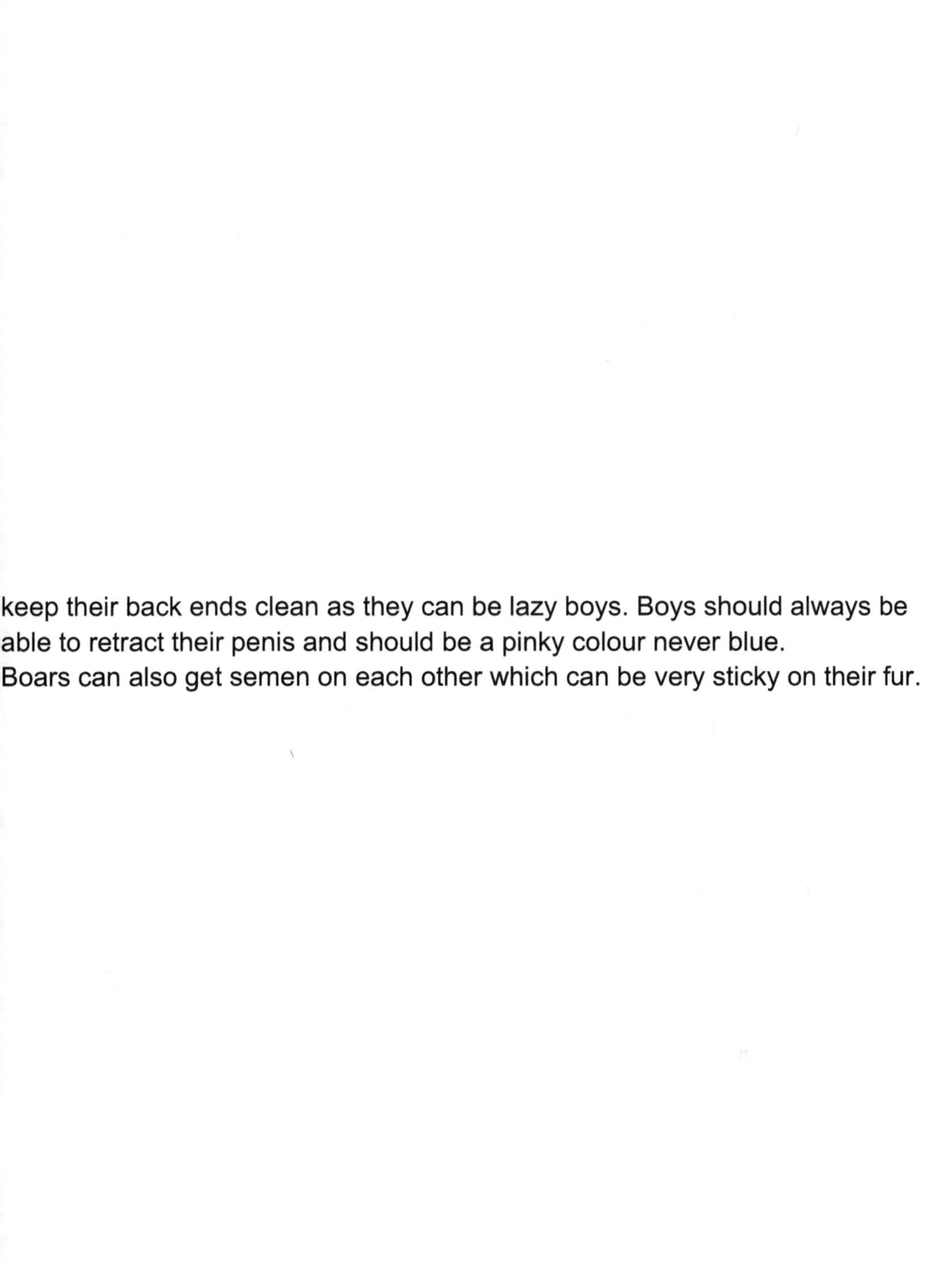

keep their back ends clean as they can be lazy boys. Boys should always be able to retract their penis and should be a pinky colour never blue.
Boars can also get semen on each other which can be very sticky on their fur.

My Guinea Pig

Date I got my Piggie(s)

Name (s)

Age

Sex

Birthday

Favourite Veg

Favourite Treats

Important Information

Weight Chart

www.ingramcontent.com/pod-product-compliance
Lightning Source LLC
LaVergne TN
LVHW020535160826
845677LV00015B/4071

9798352147139